i

Welcome

SEVENTEEN have been active in the K-pop industry for almost a decade now, and they show no signs of slowing down. Known as the "Performance Kings" of K-pop, all 13 members of the group are deeply involved in creating their music, from writing and production to choreography. Over the years, they have released several hit singles, won numerous awards and sold millions of albums – including the biggest-selling album globally in 2023. Whether you are a die-hard CARAT or a new fan, you can follow the journey of these K-pop sensations with the Ultimate Fan's Guide to SEVENTEEN!

Welcome

SEVENTEEN have been active in the K-pop industry for almost a decade now, and they show no signs of slowing down. Known as the "Performance Kings" of K-pop, all 13 members of the group are deeply involved in creating their music, from writing and production to choreography. Over the years, they have released several hit singles, won numerous awards and sold millions of albums – including the biggest-selling album globally in 2023. Whether you are a die-hard CARAT or a new fan, you can follow the journey of these K-pop sensations with the Ultimate Fan's Guide to SEVENTEEN!

S.Coups

The overall bandleader and also leader of SEVENTEEN's hip-hop unit, Choi Seung Cheol – who we know much better as S.Coups – was born in the city of Daegu on 8 August 1995. He attended the School Of Performing Arts in Korea's capital, Seoul, and then signed up at Hanyang University, where he later enrolled to do a Master's degree. After signing with Pledis Entertainment in 2010, he played a major part in the *SEVENTEEN TV* online reality show, performed with Orange Caramel and made appearances in music clips by NU'EST, Hello Venus and After School. He's a man in demand.

Jeonghan

Born in Seoul on 4 October 1995, vocal unit member Yoon Jeong Han is said to be a sensitive chap and the guy that the other SEVENTEEN musicians go to when they need to share heartache. Despite this, he loves playing pranks on his fellow SEVENTEEN-ers, and is full of energy, perhaps because he used to play football when he was a kid. The meaning of his Korean name is 'clean country', and peace of mind is important to him: he even told *INSIDE SEVENTEEN* that he likes to carry plastic spoons or chopsticks around with him because they make him feel calm. A good man to take on a picnic.

Joshua

Vocalist Joshua Hong was born in Los Angeles, USA on 30 December 1995 to South Korean parents, and was spotted by a Pledis Entertainment agent in 2013. Moving to Seoul the same year, he began idol training and joined the second season of *SEVENTEEN TV*. He released a cover of British singer dhruv's 'Double Take' in 2022 and was cast in the game show *Bro & Marble In Dubai* the following year. He didn't stop there, though, recording songs as part of Apple Music's Home Session series, hosting the company's *Summer Vacation* TV show and guesting on a remix by New Kids On The Block in 2023.

Jun

Dancer and vocalist Wen Junhui had a long career in entertainment before he joined SEVENTEEN's performance unit. Born in Shenzhen, China on 10 June 1996, he was a child actor in films such as 2007's *The Pye-Dog*, which bagged him the Hong Kong Film Directors' Guild's Best New Actor Silver Award, and *The Legend Is Born: Ip Man* three years later. Jun also appeared in TV adverts, both in Hong Kong and mainland China. He's a solo artist as well, releasing his debut single, 'Can You Sit By My Side' in December 2018, and he co-hosted a Chinese music show called *Yo! Bang* the same year.

Hoshi

The leader of SEVENTEEN's performance unit is Kwon Soon Young, born on 15 June 1996 in Namyangju. He attended Maseok High School and then enrolled in Hanyang University before signing with Pledis Entertainment in 2011. He's been busy since then, releasing his first solo music in 2021 and joining BSS while performing with SEVENTEEN. You can also see Hoshi doing his thing in the 2023 reality show *Bro & Marble In Dubai* alongside a cast of K-pop celebs: with a work ethic like this and so many different projects to keep him occupied, he is unlikely to be taking a break anytime soon.

Wonwoo

A rapper in SEVENTEEN's hip-hop unit, Jeon Won Woo looks up to S.Coups, admiring his leadership, but he has plenty of achievements on his own CV. He's a singer as well as a rap artist, he's a voracious reader and he occasionally directs videos, such as the clip for SEVENTEEN's song 'Holiday'. Born on 17 July 1996 in Changwon, he has a younger brother called Jeon Bohyuk and is a fan of idols Lupe Fiasco and Tablo. Even though he's one of SEVENTEEN's most visual characters, Wonwoo describes himself as an introvert, so you won't see him falling out of any nightclubs.

Woozi

Born in Busan on 22 November 1996, Lee Ji Hoon is a singer, songwriter and record producer, as well as the leader of SEVENTEEN's vocal unit. He studied classical music as a kid, learning the clarinet, and graduated from Hanlim Multi Art School before enrolling in Hanyang University. A friend of the producer Bumzu, he has written and produced his own music alongside that of SEVENTEEN, as well as songs by the artists Eric Nam and Baekho of NU'EST and the soundtrack of the TV series *The Tale Of Nokdu*. Most notably, he helped to write and produce every song on SEVENTEEN's debut EP, *17 CARAT*.

DK

Lee Seok Min, better known as DK, is one of SEVENTEEN's main vocalists as well as the leader of the BooSeokSoon subunit, usually referred to as BSS. In addition, he's a member of the '97 Liners squad alongside Mingyu and The8, so he's not short of friends! Born on 18 February 1997 in Mapo-gu, DK acted the main role of King Arthur in the 2019 musical *Xcalibur* and is one of the main characters in SEVENTEEN. He has talked about being responsible for the group feeling good vibes, as a friend to all the members, and admits to feeling lonely when they're not together.

Mingyu

Born on 6 April 1997 in Anyang-si, Kim Min Gyu does three jobs as the main rapper, visual and face of SEVENTEEN. He began idol training back in 2011 and appeared in videos by NU'EST before joining the band. You can also see him hanging out with SEVENTEEN's DK and The8, Jungkook from BTS, BamBam and Yugyeom from GOT7, Jaehyun from NCT and Cha Eun Woo from ASTRO in the '97 Liners, a friend group named after the members' year of birth. When he's not performing, you'll find Mingyu making art alongside The8: his first piece was titled 'Growing Pains'.

The8

Dancer and singer Xu Minghao was born in Haicheng, China on 7 November 1997 and attended Beijing Contemporary Music Academy. As early as 2008, he was seen on the Chinese programme *CCTV Variety Show*, and by 2012 he was a participant in the 6th Shanghai World Dance Competition, where he finished eighth – hence his stage name, right? After he debuted with SEVENTEEN in 2015, The8 also appeared on *Real Class – Elementary School* and on a Chinese reality television show called *Chao Yin Zhan Ji*. Space doesn't permit a full list of his credits: let's just say that the man's been busy.

Seungkwan

Born on 16 January 1998 in the same city as Woozi – Busan – Boo Seung Kwan is a singer, a member of SEVENTEEN's vocal unit, and also a member of BSS alongside Hoshi and DK. You can see him in Korean variety shows such as *Unexpected Q, Prison Life Of Fools*, and the intriguingly-titled *Idol Dictation Contest*, where he runs a parallel career as a screen presenter and entertainer. Even as a kid, Seungkwan was unstoppable when it came to performing for people, singing at song festivals held at his school: when a teacher filmed him on stage and posted it online, it led to his signing with Pledis Entertainment in 2012.

Vernon

Hansol Vernon Chwe was born on 18 February 1998 in New York, but moved with his family back to South Korea at the age of five. He was spotted nine years later and soon signed up to become a trainee with Pledis Entertainment. One of SEVENTEEN's rappers and faces, Vernon's mother is of French and German ancestry while his father is Korean. When he's not working with the band, he enjoys fashion and food from different cultures, including chocolate cakes, cheesecake and cheeseburgers. It's said that he has a large collection of hats, and why not? An idol has to rock tasty headwear.

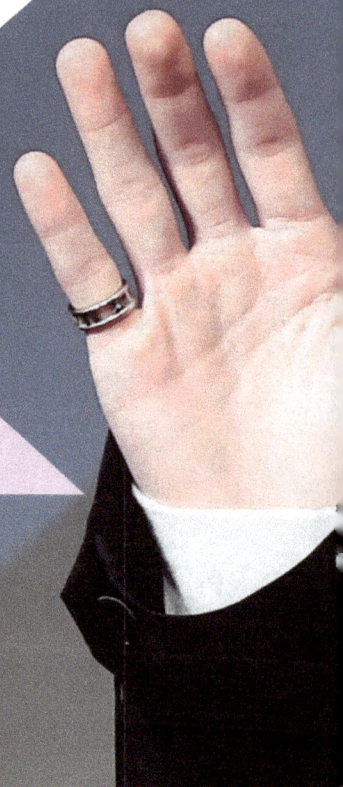

Dino

Lee Chan, born in Iksan on 11 February 1999, is a dancer, vocalist and rapper, and he's also the youngest member – the maknae – of SEVENTEEN. In retrospect, Dino was always going to be a dancer, as this noble art was popular in his family: in fact, his dad taught him how to dance. Years of dance training followed, with high placements in various competitions: he signed with Pledis Entertainment in 2012 and debuted as maknae with the band three years later. Dino is a big fan of Michael Jackson, but he also loves classical music, which he listens to when falling asleep at night.

BUILDING THE BAND

Can it really be 11 years since SEVENTEEN first appeared on our screens? We first met the gang on the Ustream reality show *SEVENTEEN TV*, which featured contestants in training for entry into the band – the original idea being that it would have 17 members. In the end, only 13 made it through, with the group split into vocal, hip-hop and performance units. The name SEVENTEEN still makes sense, though, thanks to the magic formula of '13 musicians + 3 units + 1 band = 17'. Mind, you, that's probably no consolation to the four guys who didn't make the cut!

THE BIG DEBUT

SEVENTEEN debuted on 26 May 2015 with a one-hour live showcase gig on MBC, the first male K-pop group to do so. The showcase was the finale of the *SEVENTEEN PROJECT: Debut Big Plan* TV show and was followed three days later by the first SEVENTEEN release, a digital EP titled 17 CARAT. The response was immediate, with *17 CARAT* hitting number four in Korea and eight in the USA World chart, spearheaded by the 'Adore U' single. This song was the first of a trilogy that told the eternal tale of falling in love with someone and summoning up the courage to ask them out... we've all been there.

BOYS BE

SEVENTEEN's second EP, *BOYS BE*, was released in September 2015 and made history by hitting the top spot of the US Billboard World chart, as well as making number two in Korea. Why was it such a smash hit? Possibly because the three-units concept of the band appealed to all sectors of K-pop fandom, home and abroad; maybe because the 13-member band had idols for all tastes; definitely because the songs, a mixture of love ballads and dancefloor bangers, were too good to resist. The EP has gone on to sell almost 170,000 copies in Korea alone – a sign of great things to come.

Image Alamy

WELCOME TO THE CLUB

By 2016, SEVENTEEN's ever-growing fandom needed a group to call their own, so the band set up a poll for six possible fan club names – Tinker Bell, Tinvely, Wish, Same, Wennie and CARAT. On 14 February, the winning name was announced by S.Coups at the LIKE SEVENTEEN: Boys Wish gig, saying "You guys made us shine so bright, so you guys are now going to be our CARAT". The club's official colours of rose quartz and serenity were then revealed, with a CARAT lightstick available to buy in multiple formats. Eight membership recruitments have taken place each year since then.

LOVE & LETTER

In April 2016, SEVENTEEN released their debut studio album, *LOVE&LETTER*, which hit high on no fewer than three American charts, topped the Korean list and also made number eight on the Japanese weekly charts – the last of these achievements significant because the group had yet to debut in that country. A single, 'Pretty U', led off the campaign and was warmly received by the fandom. Three months later, the album was reissued as *Love&Letter repackage album*, with the addition of five bonus tracks, 'NO F.U.N', 'Healing', 'SIMPLE', 'Space' and the single 'VERY NICE' – which became another major hit.

GOING SEVENTEEN

SEVENTEEN signalled the arrival of their third EP – *Going Seventeen* – in December 2016 with the single 'BOOMBOOM', a suitably floor-weakening slab of urban music. It helped the EP head to the top of the Korean charts and to number three in the USA, where SEVENTEEN's fanbase was rapidly on the rise. The eight new songs on the EP gave the fandom a welcome boost just before the group headed to Japan in early 2017 for the '17 JAPAN CONCERT: Say the name #SEVENTEEN' tour, where thousands of rapturous fans lined up to hear all of the things.

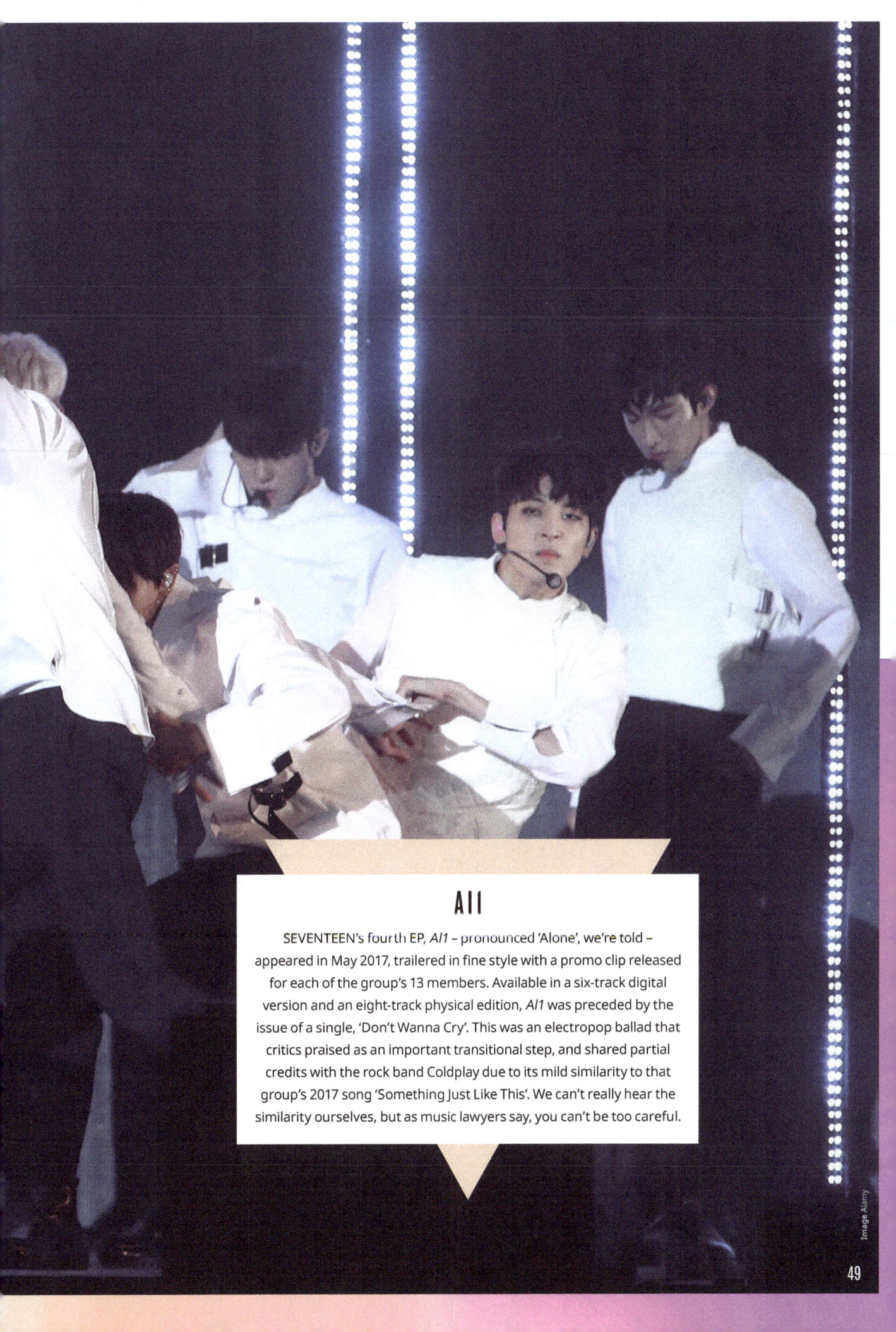

Al1

SEVENTEEN's fourth EP, *Al1* – pronounced 'Alone', we're told – appeared in May 2017, trailered in fine style with a promo clip released for each of the group's 13 members. Available in a six-track digital version and an eight-track physical edition, *Al1* was preceded by the issue of a single, 'Don't Wanna Cry'. This was an electropop ballad that critics praised as an important transitional step, and shared partial credits with the rock band Coldplay due to its mild similarity to that group's 2017 song 'Something Just Like This'. We can't really hear the similarity ourselves, but as music lawyers say, you can't be too careful.

TEEN, AGE

SEVENTEEN album number two – *TEEN, AGE*, pronounced with a short pause at its midpoint – was unleashed onto the CARAT fandom and beyond in November 2017, helped along nicely by a stadium-friendly song called 'CLAP'. A special version of the album titled *Director's Cut* featured the same tracks as TEEN, AGE plus four new songs on its release in February 2018, the new cuts being 'Thinkin' about you', 'THANKS', 'Run to you' and 'Falling For U'. American, Japanese and domestic fans rewarded the album with high chart positions. Could anything stop the progress of SEVENTEEN now?

YOU MAKE MY DAY

What do you do if you're on tour when your platinum-selling fifth EP is released? Why, do press interviews between shows, of course. Exhausting though it undoubtedly was, when SEVENTEEN released *YOU MAKE MY DAY* in July 2018, they were playing shows in Seoul under the IDEAL CUT banner as well as travelling for overseas concerts. The EP's six tracks included the single 'Oh My!' and were snapped up by the fandom, who propelled *YOU MAKE MY DAY* (presumably not inspired by the classic *Dirty Harry* line) to number one in Korea and 500,000 sales.

YOU MADE MY DAWN

EP number six, *YOU MADE MY DAWN*, appeared in January 2019 – but doesn't 'Dawn' usually come before 'Day'? The fans weren't worried about this glitch in the SEVENTEEN matrix, and bought the EP in droves. Two singles, 'Getting Closer' and 'Home', spread the message further, with the former described as 'dark hip-hop' and the latter as 'future bass', a style of electronic music influenced by dubstep and trap. Musically, SEVENTEEN were expanding their range, and fortunately, it seemed that the fandom was with them every step of the way. Where were they headed? Let's find out…

Image Getty Images

An

SEVENTEEN

AN ODE

Four years into their careers, the members of SEVENTEEN were evolving, and this was evident in the sound of their third studio album, *An Ode*, released in September 2019, not long before the pandemic put everything on hold for a while. "We expressed our inner fears this time... We will continue to try to show newer sides of ourselves," co-producer Woozi told MTV, and indeed the songs were a little darker than on previous releases. Still, the singles 'HIT' and 'Fear' had a ton of energy despite their more mature themes, and *An Ode* was a hit in the usual places, as well as making inroads in France and Poland.

TOURING THE WORLD

Too busy to go and see SEVENTEEN play a show in Korea or Japan? No worries – just wait for them to come to your hometown. That's exactly what they did in 2017 with the DIAMOND EDGE tour, two years later with the ODE TO YOU jaunt and in 2022 with the BE THE SUN run of dates. The first included US dates as well as East Asian shows for a 14-date run, and the second added a Mexico show that netted over $750,000. Two years ago, the BE THE SUN dates grossed over $43m and sold 440,000 tickets, even though there were only 12 shows. That's entertainment!

HENG:GARÆ

On 22 June 2020, SEVENTEEN released *Heng:garæ*, their seventh EP – and promptly sold a million copies in less than a week. It hit the top of the Japanese charts and, even more impressively, topped the iTunes Top Album charts in 27 countries worldwide. So why was it such a smash hit? Probably because its two singles, 'My My' and 'Left & Right', were fun dancefloor-fillers, but also because SEVENTEEN's time in the international spotlight had arrived with a vengeance. From this point on, our 13 merry men were no longer run-of-the-mill K-pop idols – they were superstars.

; [SEMICOLON]

Either an EP or a 'special album' depending on which source you consult, *; [Semicolon]* was released on 19 October 2020 and blew all our minds with the news that a million copies had been pre-ordered before it hit the shelves. Bear in mind that it came out only four months after *Heng:garæ*, itself a million-seller: clearly, the fandom couldn't get enough of SEVENTEEN. Not that the group were treading water – the new songs included elements of funk, acid jazz and even bossa nova for the first time. SEVENTEEN promoted the new release with a ton of socially-distanced TV shows, this being the height of the pandemic.

YOUR CHOICE

Stepping up their game into disco and R&B territory, SEVENTEEN released *Your Choice* in June 2021. Its lyrics were at least partly designed to cheer up the CARAT fandom, deprived of seeing their idols in person by COVID-19: as Seungkwan explained, "We thought the message of love is what could really console people and resonate with them, especially in these tough times that we're having". The public liked this idea and *Your Choice* became SEVENTEEN's third million-seller in a row, promoted by performances on Korean and US TV: it also scored highly on charts in 11 countries around the world.

SEVENTEEN

9TH MINI ALBU

ATTACCA

EP number nine appeared in 2021 – and guess what, it sold not one but two million copies. *Attacca*, as it was called, came with a fully-leaded concept that the SEVENTEEN fandom thoroughly enjoyed, beginning with an apocalyptic video. When the word 'boyhood' appeared on the screen followed by a teddy bear in flames, fans speculated that *Attacca*'s theme would be about evolution – and so it proved to be. A medley of song snippets helped to build excitement before the release, a solid idea as the EP hit two million in sales inside three months.

ATTACCA

FACE T

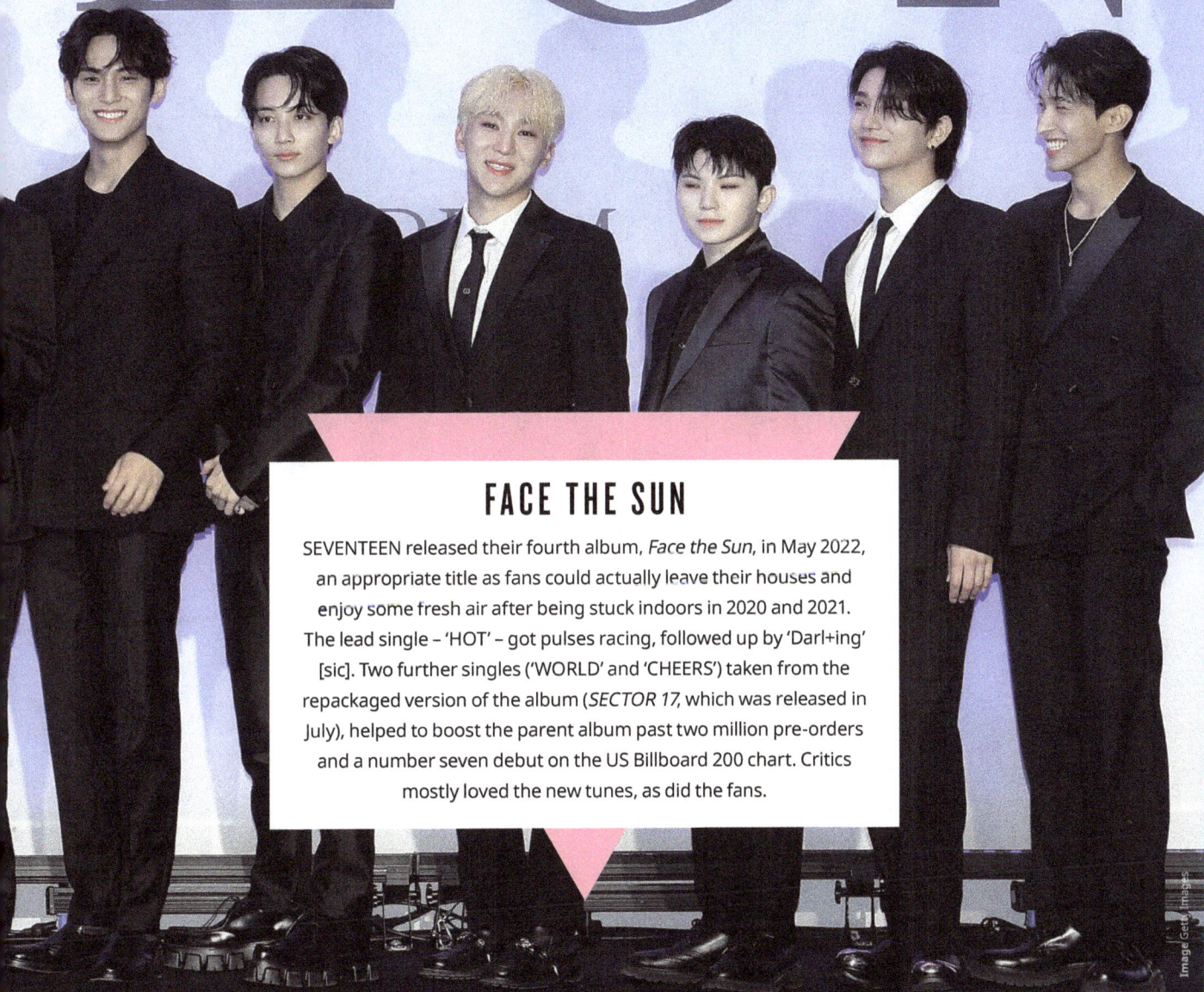

FACE THE SUN

SEVENTEEN released their fourth album, *Face the Sun*, in May 2022, an appropriate title as fans could actually leave their houses and enjoy some fresh air after being stuck indoors in 2020 and 2021. The lead single – 'HOT' – got pulses racing, followed up by 'Darl+ing' [sic]. Two further singles ('WORLD' and 'CHEERS') taken from the repackaged version of the album (*SECTOR 17*, which was released in July), helped to boost the parent album past two million pre-orders and a number seven debut on the US Billboard 200 chart. Critics mostly loved the new tunes, as did the fans.

AWARDS IN JAPAN

THE STAR
PARTNER

SMBC 三井住友銀行
V POINT

STARNEWS

KRONOS

HITO-com

STARNEWS

TAG·COFFEE STAN(D)

MEDIABOY

Life de YUI

SP CARE

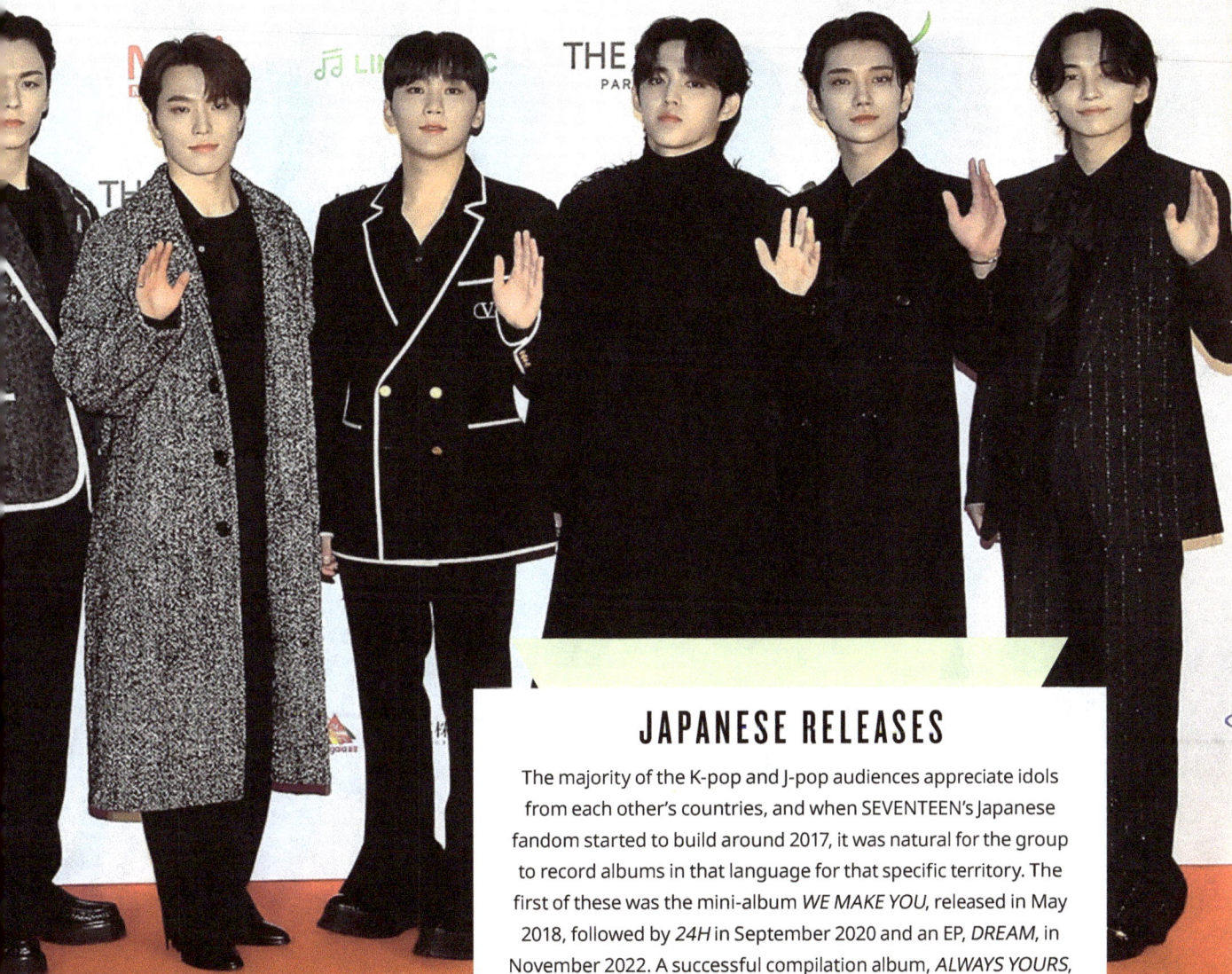

JAPANESE RELEASES

The majority of the K-pop and J-pop audiences appreciate idols from each other's countries, and when SEVENTEEN's Japanese fandom started to build around 2017, it was natural for the group to record albums in that language for that specific territory. The first of these was the mini-album *WE MAKE YOU*, released in May 2018, followed by *24H* in September 2020 and an EP, *DREAM*, in November 2022. A successful compilation album, *ALWAYS YOURS*, followed a year later and ensured that SEVENTEEN will always have a home away from home in the Land of the Rising Sun.

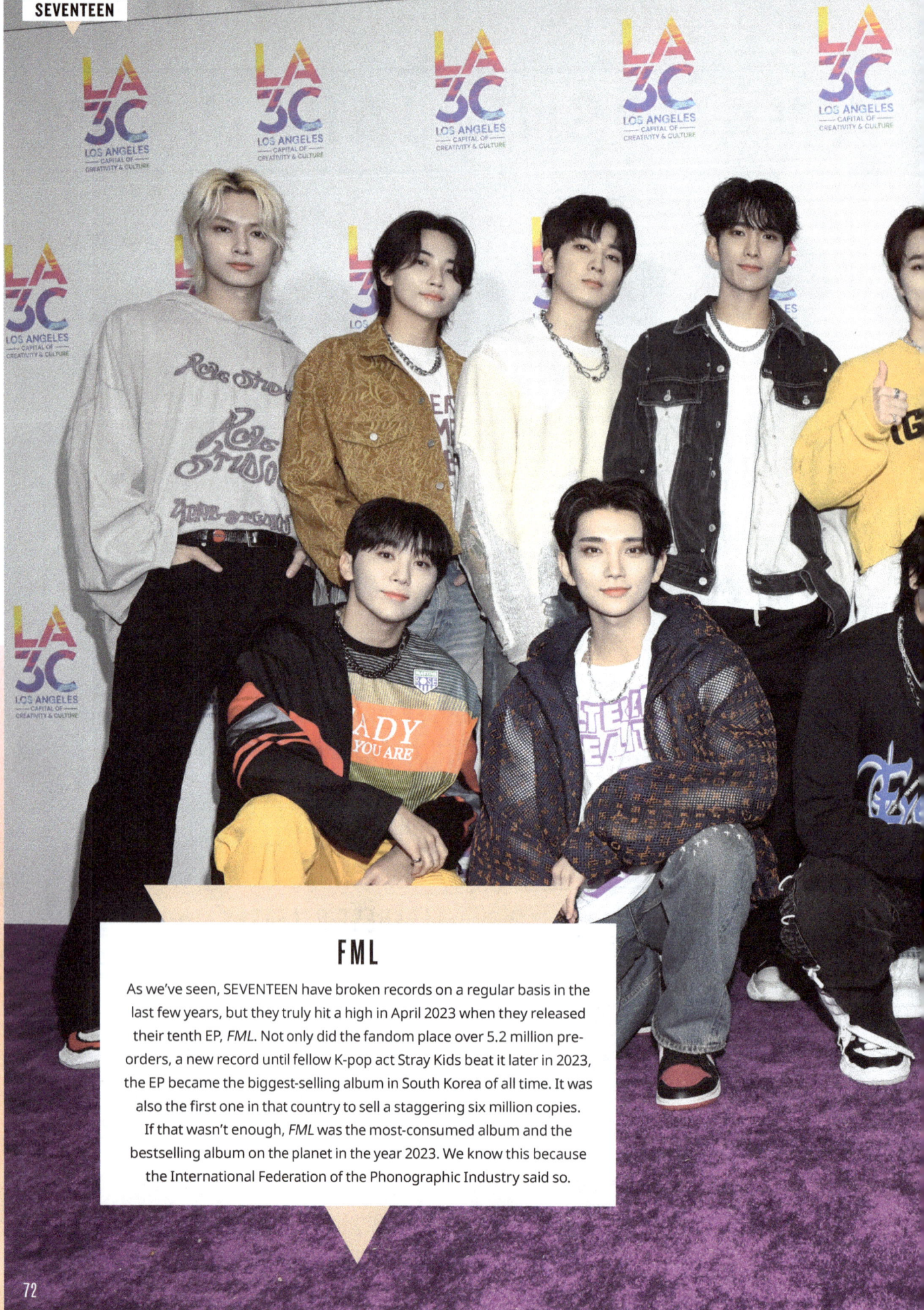

FML

As we've seen, SEVENTEEN have broken records on a regular basis in the last few years, but they truly hit a high in April 2023 when they released their tenth EP, *FML*. Not only did the fandom place over 5.2 million pre-orders, a new record until fellow K-pop act Stray Kids beat it later in 2023, the EP became the biggest-selling album in South Korea of all time. It was also the first one in that country to sell a staggering six million copies.

If that wasn't enough, *FML* was the most-consumed album and the bestselling album on the planet in the year 2023. We know this because the International Federation of the Phonographic Industry said so.

2023 MAMA A

SEVENTEENTH HEAVEN

Eleven EPs into their career, you might think that SEVENTEEN and their handlers would be running out of ideas – but with *SEVENTEENTH HEAVEN*, released on 23 October 2023, the opposite was shown to be the case. A dance-heavy collection led off by the single 'God of Music', the EP also featured the US producer Marshmello on 'SOS' and was greeted with an astounding 5.2 million pre-orders, the most in history. The marketing campaign included pop-up events throughout Korea, although the band's label, Pledis Entertainment, had to apologise to the Chinese fandom, who protested when an image of that country's Great Wall was depicted in the promo campaign.

DOING GOOD

SEVENTEEN have always supported charitable causes. We can't fit a full list in here, but organisations such as Korea's Social Welfare Society's 'Letters from Angels' campaign, ChildFund Korea, Plastic Bank, the humanitarian NGO Good Neighbors and Korea's Global Education Sharing Project are among them. Along the way, band members have donated collectively and individually, designed and signed garments and artworks to sell, and given supportive speeches. An example of the latter came in November 2023 when the group performed at UNESCO HQ in France to encourage awareness and fundraising, becoming the first K-pop band to do so.

17 IS RIGHT HERE

On 29 April 2024, SEVENTEEN released their third compilation album and the second in their native language, *17 IS RIGHT HERE*. Collecting every Korean-language single they've released in their nine-year career so far, the double CD also included Korean versions of the group's Japanese-language singles, as well as the group's new title track, 'MAESTRO'. A dance R&B song composed by Woozi and others, 'MAESTRO' was positively received and the group first performed it at their 'FOLLOW' AGAIN TO SEOUL concerts on 27 and 28 April. Now all we need is a compilation of English-language re-recordings...

WHAT'S NEXT?

What's the biggest musical festival in the UK? Glastonbury, of course, and this long-running cultural institution reminded us of its forward-thinking nature in 2024 by announcing that its first-ever K-pop headliner would be SEVENTEEN. Our favourite baker's dozen will be taking the stage in June alongside Dua Lipa, Coldplay, SZA, Shania Twain, LCD Soundsystem, PJ Harvey and others before heading off to play Lollapalooza in Berlin in September, making up a cancelled pandemic date. Is there any more proof required of SEVENTEEN's cultural impact in the West? We think not. See you in the front row...

ULTIMATE FAN'S GUIDE TO

SEVENTEEN

Future PLC Quay House, The Ambury, Bath, BA1 1UA

Editorial
Editor **Jessica Leggett**
Art Editor **Thomas Parrett**
Head of Art & Design **Greg Whitaker**
Editorial Director **Jon White**
Managing Director **Grainne McKenna**

Contributors
Dave Smith, Jo Cole

Cover images
Getty Images, Alamy

Photography
All copyrights and trademarks are recognised and respected

Advertising
Media packs are available on request
Commercial Director **Clare Dove**

International
Head of Print Licensing **Rachel Shaw**
licensing@futurenet.com
www.futurecontenthub.com

Circulation
Head of Newstrade **Tim Mathers**

Production
Head of Production **Mark Constance**
Production Project Manager **Matthew Eglinton**
Advertising Production Manager **Joanne Crosby**
Digital Editions Controller **Jason Hudson**
Production Managers **Keely Miller, Nola Cokely,
Vivienne Calvert, Fran Twentyman**

Ultimate Fan's Guide to SEVENTEEN (MUB6306)
© 2024 Future Publishing Limited

FUTURE Connectors.
Creators.
Experience
Makers.

Future plc is a public   Chief Executive Officer **Jon Steinberg**
company quoted on the   Non-Executive Chairman **Richard Huntingford**
London Stock Exchange   Chief Financial and Strategy Officer **Penny Ladkin-Brand**
(symbol: FUTR)
www.futureplc.com   Tel +44 (0)1225 442 244